HOSKIN BOOKS ON WORSHIP AND MISSION

Into the Household of God

A presider's manual for the rite of Baptism in the Book of Alternative Services

John W. B. Hill

Illustrated by Willem Hart

This book is published under a grant from the St. James Westminster Foundation

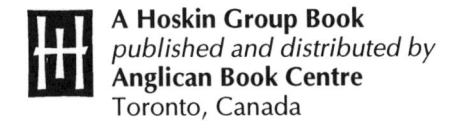

A Hoskin Group Book
published and distributed by
Anglican Book Centre
Toronto, Canada

© 1994, The Hoskin Group

A HOSKIN GROUP BOOK

Published and distributed by
ANGLICAN BOOK CENTRE
600 Jarvis Street, Toronto, Ontario M4Y 2J6 Canada

All rights reserved. No part of this publication may be reproduced, transmitted, transcribed, stored in a retrieval system, or translated into any language in any form by any means without the written permission of The Hoskin Group.

Typesetting, design & illustration: Willem Hart

Every effort has been made to obtain copyright on original text, photography, and other illustrations. Where we have erred, please contact the publisher.

The Hoskin Group is a society committed to the ongoing renewal of the Church in worship and mission. Our ministry is to provide resources which focus the debate, inform the practice, and evaluate the experience of our liturgical life.

Books Committee: David Holeton, Maud McLean, Matthew Johnson

Canadian Cataloguing in Publication Data

   Hill, John W. B. (John William Barnabas), 1944-
     Into the Household of God

   ISBN 1-55126-087-5

   1. Baptism – Anglican Church of Canada. 2. Baptism
   (Liturgy). 3. Anglican Church of Canada. Book of alternative services of the
   Anglican Church of Canada. I. Title.

   BX5616.H55 1994   264'.0351   C94-931151-0

TABLE OF CONTENTS

Preface	5
Introduction	9
Preparing for the liturgy	27
Celebrating the liturgy	33
The gathering and proclamation of the Word	34
The presentation and examination of the candidates	36
The celebration of baptism	41
The celebration of the eucharist	53
Appendices	
1 Resources	55
2 Music	59
3 Intercessions	64
4 The giving of the new clothes	66
5 Reflection on the experience of immersion	67
6 Baptismal pools	68
7 Preaching at baptism	73

*We receive you into the household of God.
Confess the faith of Christ crucified,
proclaim his resurrection,
and share with us in his eternal priesthood.*

Holy Baptism, *Book of Alternative Services*, page 161.

PREFACE

The Hoskin Group undertakes to provide a series of practical and thought-provoking manuals for those who must plan and celebrate the rites of the Book of Alternative Services. *Let Us Give Thanks*, the first in this series, offered directions for celebrating the BAS eucharist; and its instructions are appropriately straightforward.

A manual on baptism, however, cannot be so straightforward. Whereas the eucharist has moved increasingly to the centre of our life in recent years, the recovery of the centrality of baptism has hardly begun. Over the past centuries baptism became so marginalized that its increasingly shrivelled ritual came to bear little resemblance to the symbolic vigour of its origins.

Writing a manual on baptism presents a dilemma, then. Should it offer suggestions for tidying up an admittedly defective ritual? Or should it try to demonstrate what a restored ritual would actually look like?

The latter course has been chosen, in the full knowledge that this may prove an obstacle for some readers. Obviously, there is no quick and easy path from where we are to where we might dream of being; and readers will have to pick and choose those elements of a restored ritual which seem physically and pastorally feasible.

Nevertheless, the time has come for all of us to begin dreaming together about ways of celebrating baptism that will bear the weight of our baptismal theology. This manual is offered in the hope that it may help to stir such dreams in the Anglican Church of Canada.

In view of this ambitious hope, the introductory section is obliged to explore at length some of the practical problems we face. This is followed by suggestions for preparing for the liturgy, even though true 'preparation' would carry us far beyond the scope of this manual. Finally, there is a detailed account of the celebration itself. A number of appendices offer resources and side-lights on various aspects of baptismal celebration.

Special thanks are due to those who contributed to this work: James Belli who contributed photographs; Willem Hart who designed and illustrated the manual; Shirley Griffin who wrote about her own experience of baptism; and fellow members of the Hoskin Group who offered constructive criticism along the way. Needless to say, the author alone bears responsibility for the limitations of the final product.

John W. B. Hill
Toronto, March 1994

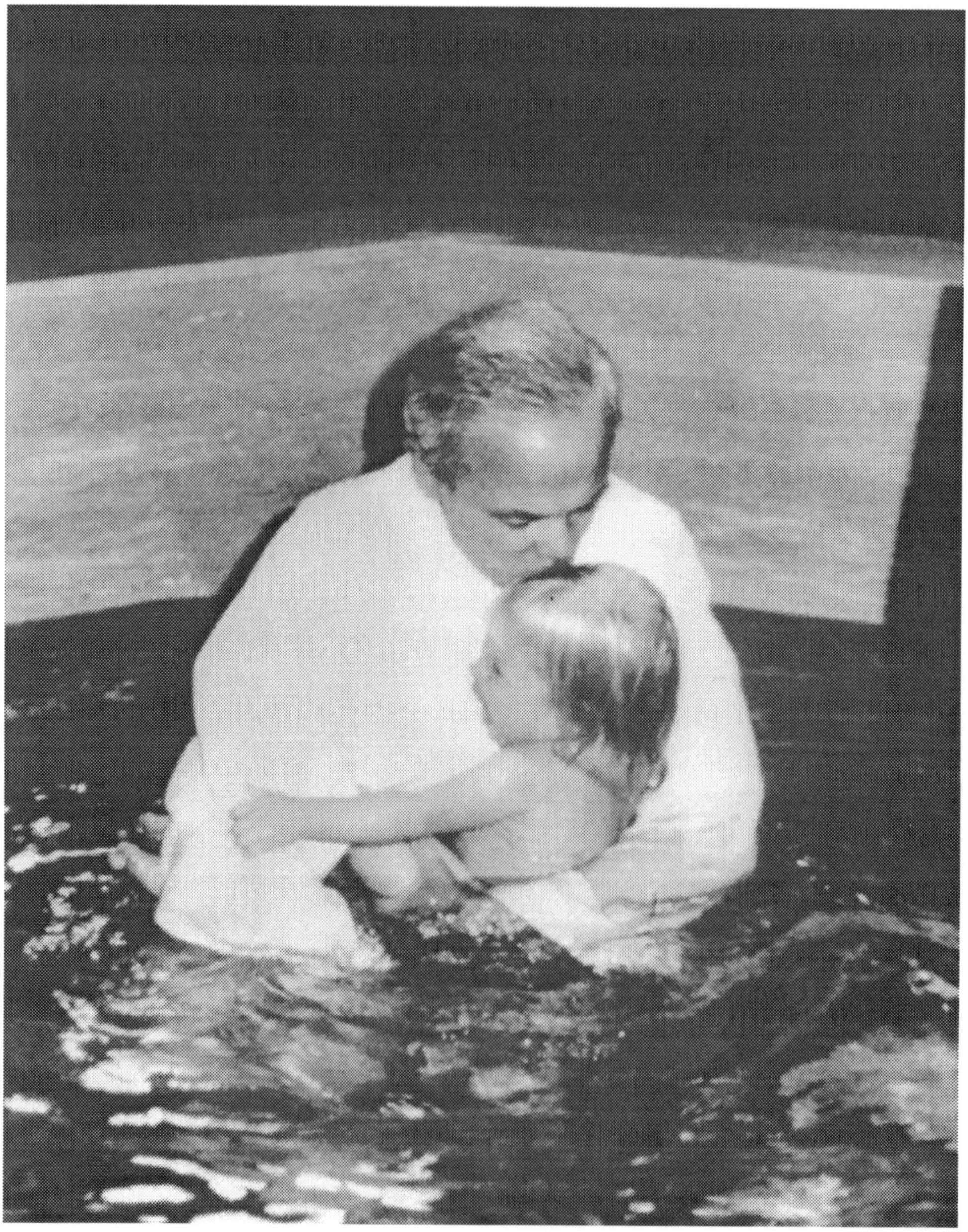

INTRODUCTION

Baptism is the sacramental wellspring of our corporate life in Christ. It is the continuing genesis of the Church; for by baptism God incorporates humanity, one by one, into the paschal mystery of Jesus Christ, dead and risen, into the body of which Christ is the head. In baptism we discover who we are as God's new creation, the people of the new covenant in Jesus Christ, the community of the Holy Spirit.

Celebrating baptism with verve and integrity is therefore of the utmost importance, for if we fail at this point we shall forget who and what we are; we shall forget our sacred calling. It is not surprising that Christian communities which have pushed baptism to the margins of their life are having increasing difficulty defining and cultivating life in Christ. They seek to justify their existence by their good works, and aspire to nothing higher than their own survival. They forget that "those who want to save their life will lose it." It is only communities which know how to receive life as a gift from God — by giving it away — that will be saved.

One of the ways we have marginalized baptism is by dislocating it from its proper connection with the gospel (its progenitor) and with communion in love (its progeny). Many candidates for baptism have never really heard that there is good news, and many never seek their place in the communion of the faithful. When it is disconnected in these ways, baptism loses its power and purpose; presider and congregation alike begin to exhibit apathy or annoyance with baptismal celebration.

This dislocation has also made it easier for us to trivialize the ritual, and render its great symbols innocuous. Any attempt today to recognize in our tidy conventional ceremony the awesome, traditional images of baptism will surely end in dismay: turning from idols to serve the living God? new creation in Christ? death and resurrection? adoption into a new family? rebirth in Holy Spirit? So little of all this remains. We are left instead with a birth ritual, a naming ceremony.

Moreover, now that baptism is once again becoming a public celebration, a new set of problems has been emerging. Some congregations are increasingly cynical about baptism, offended by the repeated experience of liturgical lying. How can faithful Christians respond to the question, "Will you do all in your power to support these persons in their new life in Christ?" when they have never seen them before and do not expect to see them again? Other congregations are realizing for the first time that the number of baptisms is out of all proportion to the actual growth of the church; and, in spite of their best intentions, they cannot cope with the emotional weight of all these solemn 'initiations', many of whom, they assume will be 'still births'. There are even congregations whose members stay home on baptism Sundays because they feel alienated by the intrusion into community worship of what appear to be private family affairs.

Behind these problems lies a tangle of confused notions about baptism and what it does. It is time for us to wake up and recognize that baptism has been sabotaged by folk custom and ecclesiastical negligence. Baptism has become for many people an end in itself; and many of those who ask for it already have fixed ideas about it, based not upon what the rite says or what the church teaches, but upon the sentimental practices to which they are accustomed. Nothing we do to strengthen liturgical language will change these ideas; only the restoration of a sound catechumenal ministry of formation as *part of the process of initiation* will make a difference (see *Making Disciples*, also published in this series, and listed in Appendix 1).

Baptism must be seen as just one of several elements in a regenerative cycle in the life of the Church — a Church which is itself a sacrament of God's transforming reign within the world. Hearing the gospel leads to baptism into the divine/human communion; this enables life in the Spirit in the midst of the life of the world; the signs of this new life create a hearing for the gospel; and this leads to baptism into communion, which enables life in the Spirit, and so on...(Diagram 1). But the cycle is broken when baptism is offered for any other reason than response to the gospel. The cycle is also broken when communion becomes self-love, and fails to issue in a life of service to the world. The cycle is broken when the world is served in the power of any other motive than the love born of communion. The cycle is broken when proclamation becomes propaganda, not waiting for the hearing created by faithful life in the Spirit.

Reconnecting Baptism to Gospel and vocation

This manual, therefore, is a plea for integrity,

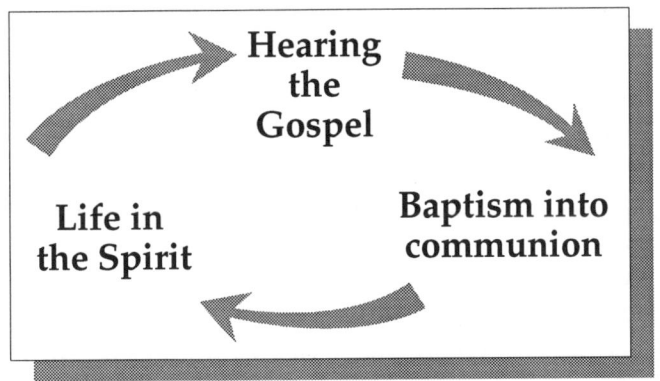

Hearing the Gospel → **Baptism into communion** → **Life in the Spirit** → (cycle continues)

for the dynamic wholeness of this regenerative cycle of divine life poured out for the life of the world. Such integrity cannot be achieved merely by strengthening the ritual; and Anglicans around the world are beginning to see in the catechumenate a model for reforming baptismal practice (see *Growing in Newness of Life*, listed in Appendix 1, which records the work and findings of the fourth International Anglican Liturgical Consultation and commends the restored catechumenate). It will be important, however, once we *do* rise to this challenge, to have a ritual that is strong enough to support our renewed understanding of baptism.

Norms for celebrating baptism

The kind of gospel we communicate will depend critically upon the use we make of the symbols God has entrusted to us; and so we must allow them to speak with all their depth and power. Faithfulness to the gospel entails more than clinging to a minimal expression of the divine mysteries. The rite in the Book of Alternative Services may be understood as the Church's current account of the norm for administering the sacrament. According to this norm baptism is celebrated by a baptizing community; baptism is celebrated within the eucharist, on the occasion of one of the Church's principal festivals (preferably at the Great Vigil of Easter); baptism is celebrated with plenty of water (preferably by immersion); baptism is administered only to people who have sponsors within the community. Although none of these conditions are essential for valid baptism, all of them are needed for an effectual proclamation by the Church of the meaning of this sacrament entrusted to us. We need to know what constitutes valid baptism, baptism which must be recognized as such by the Church; but we must not confuse minimally valid baptism with the normative celebration of baptism. We must guard against any reduction of the depth or scope of this proclamation.

One of the most important baptismal symbols, we are now realizing, is the symbol of the baptizing community itself, the community of the covenant. The BAS rite has given this symbol new prominence by locating the Baptismal Covenant immediately prior to the baptismal washing, and making it something to be affirmed, not just by the candidates and sponsors, but by the whole congregation. The five additional questions that follow the Creed have opened our eyes to the communal implications of our baptismal profession. If we can recover a biblical sense of covenant, and allow this act of covenanting to define what we mean by 'Church', we shall discover a corporate life in the Spirit that is more than adequate for the challenges of the third millennium. Above all, we shall find that we can initiate people into a distinctively communal faith.

The covenant community

The rite of baptism in the BAS stands in a long and evolving tradition of Anglican initiatory rites which are themselves part of an even larger ritual history. The earliest Anglican forms did not escape the decadence of the medieval rites; but they did contain the vestigial remains of an earlier wisdom long forgotten, traces of the ancient catechumenate. Even these trace elements were removed in subsequent revisions; and the rite of baptism became steadily weaker until, by the late 1960s the trial rite of the Church of England (widely used in Canada) was sufficiently innocuous to sanction the most casual Sunday afternoon baptisms. Even the baptismal creed had been pruned!

But over the last few decades the Church has been awakening to the realization that accommodation is betrayal; and our current rite is a newly strengthened thing of beauty and wonder, a rite which declares in unmistakable terms what it means to be a disciple of Christ and a responsible member of his body, the Church. Unmistakable, that is, unless our *actions* betray it; changing words alone will accomplish very little. We need to rethink the shape of our baptismal *actions*.

Sponsors There are two aspects of the normative practice of baptism for which many of us still find ourselves unprepared. One is the use of sponsors in more than a nominal fashion. In order to be effective, a sponsor must be known among the baptizing community as its faithful representative. Sponsors must have the freedom and authority to fulfil the responsibility entrusted to them. Godparents may be a nice idea, but rarely do they qualify as effective sponsors. The notes that follow presuppose the recovery of this vital ministry; and those seeking guidance in this recovery may wish to consult Appendix 1 for relevant resources.

Immersion The other aspect of the normative practice of baptism is immersion. In this the BAS is no different from any previous Anglican prayer book: they all expected immersion (or 'dipping') while allowing pouring as an alternative ('sprinkling' has never even been mentioned). Until our 1962 Book of Common Prayer softened the rubrics, immersion was urged even more strongly. We simply paid no attention.

This raises a host of issues. Although a few of our fonts may actually be large enough to dip an infant (or to hold a sitting infant, so as to enable pouring water over the child's body), even this size of font fails to proclaim the truth about baptism: its size suggests that infants are the normative candidates. If there is a normative age for baptism, the BAS implies that it is not infancy but an age at which candidates can

> ¶ *Then the Prieſt ſhall take the Child into his hands, and ſhall ſay to the Godfathers and Godmothers.*
>
> Name this Child.
>
> *And then Naming it after them (if they ſhall cirtifie him that the Child may well endure it) he ſhall dip it in the Water diſcreetly and warily, ſaying,*
>
> N. I baptize thee In the Name of the Father, and of the Son, and of the Holy Ghoſt. Amen.
>
> ¶ *But if they certifie that the Child is weak, it ſhall ſuffice to pour Water upon it, ſaying the foreſaid words,*
>
> N. I baptize thee In the Name of the Father, and of the Son, and of the Holy Ghoſt. Amen.

actually *ask* for baptism. While affirming the propriety of baptizing those children who will be brought up in the community of faith, we must not allow ourselves to forget that this is an extension of the practice of baptizing those who speak for themselves, as the Presentation (p. 153) makes clear. This is something our fonts need to make clear, too.

Worse still, some parishes have been in the habit of ignoring the font and using an even smaller finger bowl placed on a table at the front of the room. This is usually done on the grounds that people need to be able to see it; the assumption is that people are doomed by those intractable pews to face in one direction, like an audience facing a stage.

Diagram 1.
The earliest example known of a building for Christian worship (a house-church in Dura-Europos on the Euphrates) contains the remains of the font (or pool).

The earliest example known to us of a building for Christian worship (a house-church in Dura-Europos on the Euphrates) has not preserved an altar or pulpit; but it does contain the remains of the font (or pool). This stands to reason: in most houses, tables and chairs are portable and replaceable, and only the bathroom fixtures stay behind when we move. Any font worthy of the name is bound to be massive; and yet in modern church furnishing only the font is trivial enough to be portable; everything *else* is usually fastened down! We need to recover the original symbolism of water in our midst (with running fountains, whenever possible). We do not need any more portable fonts. See Appendix 6 for examples.

The traditional name for such a pool was 'piscina' — a fish pond. In the third century

Tertullian wrote, "we little fishes, named thus after our great Fish, Jesus Christ, were born in water; and only by remaining in water can we live" (*On Baptism*). The Greek word 'fish' (ΙΧΘΥΣ) was by then a popular acronym for 'Jesus Christ, Son of God, Saviour' (Ιησους Χριστος Θεου Υιος Σωτηρ).

The traditional shapes of baptismal pools bear eloquent testimony to the paschal character of baptism. Sometimes they have been cruciform or tomb shaped; for "we have been buried with him by baptism into his death" (Romans 6.4). Sometimes they have been octagonal, in witness to the Christian awareness of living in the 'eighth day', the day of resurrection, the day outside the ordinary cycle of days, the beginning of the new creation, the new time of redemption; for "you have been raised with Christ" (Colossians 3.1).

Birth images only began to predominate in the design of fonts (often in the form of womb-shaped vessels) when infants came to be the usual candidates and fonts ceased to be pools suitable for all ages. Withered and desiccated like so many of our Christian symbols, the 'piscina' eventually became a sanctified drain hole for disposiing of water used in ablutions at the eucharist. But symbols can be rehabilitated! (See Appendix 6 for some contemporary examples.)

Immersion pools

A redesigned font/pool would include a basin at least 60 cm deep, and at least 120 cm broad (thus enabling a kneeling adult candidate, by bending forward, to be virtually engulfed in water); it might also include a small stream or fountain running into it ('living water'). If the water level is so low that dipping an infant becomes difficult, the pool may need to have a rim that is broad enough to sit on while dipping an infant; or a smaller elevated pool might be

Diagram 2

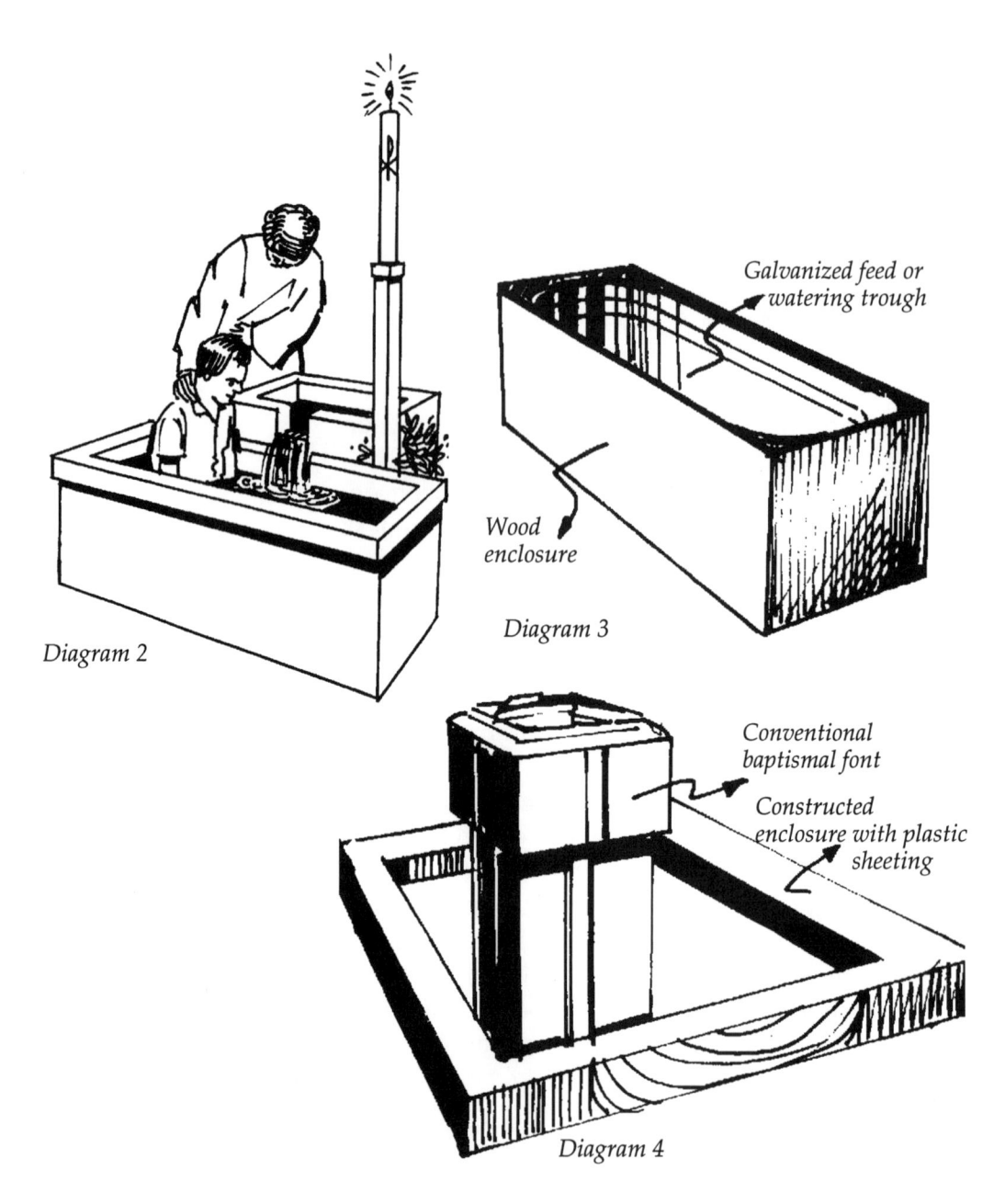

Galvanized feed or watering trough

Wood enclosure

Diagram 3

Conventional baptismal font

Constructed enclosure with plastic sheeting

Diagram 4

included, which could itself be the fountain or source of the stream. (See Diagram 2 and Appendix 6.)

A cruciform pool might fittingly have a water level that is below the level of the floor, in order to make clear that candidates go down into the water, descending into death. Some settings, of course, prohibit this on structural grounds; and a tomb-shaped pool needs to sit *upon* the floor in order to proclaim its message clearly. This requires candidates to climb in rather than step down. The ideal pool will also provide for entering the water on one side and leaving by the opposite side, so that candidates do not merely venture in like a swimmer but 'pass over'.

Such an installation needs to be served by both hot and cold water so that the water at baptism can be cool, not cold; a drainage system is also necessary. If 'living water' is part of the design, a circulating pump will be necessary; and a filtering system will help reduce the required frequency of water change.

Whatever its form, the font or pool is best left visible at all times as a continuing sign of our new birth, rather than being hidden under a cover. A pool at floor level may require movable barriers when it is not in use to prevent accidents.

Improvisation may be a necessary interim step before communities consider permanent alteration of existing baptismal facilities, and until people catch the spirit of a renewed celebration of baptism. Anyone who has tried to strengthen the symbolism of liturgical space knows the importance of trial use, and fonts are no exception. We may find ourselves for a time resorting to *temporary* fonts. But this is only appropriate when the temporary font makes a stronger (not a weaker) statement about the nature of baptism than the inherited font did.

Here are two possibilities:
1. A pool of the specified dimensions can be improvised with the help of a farm supply outlet: a galvanized feed or watering trough has proven adequate on occasion. Alternatively, a rectangular pool can be built out of wood and lined with builders' plastic sheeting, or coated inside with sealant (Diagram 3).

2. A catch-basin to enable a genuine affusion, pouring water over the whole body, is easily created by draping builders' plastic sheeting over a low-sided enclosure (kneelers have sometimes been used to create this); and the existing font can be stood beside (or inside) this enclosure. A pitcher or ewer can then be used to scoop water from the font to pour over a candidate who stands erect. Alternatively, a child's wading pool will do; this will be more presentable if lined with a white sheet (Diagram 4).

To ask candidates (or their parents) whether they would like baptism by immersion is not a good idea; for it suggests that they must judge whether such an 'extreme measure' is legitimate. Immersion is in fact no more extreme than using real bread for the eucharist; it is the legitimate and traditional practice of the Church. Better that the method of baptism be described to them well ahead of time, providing them ample opportunity to raise their questions.

Baptismal clothing

Baptism by immersion (or by real affusion) raises other practical issues. It has become the unfortunate custom for parents to bring infant candidates to their baptism already arrayed in white baptismal clothes. This defaces the original symbolism of baptismal garments — and it becomes perfectly obvious when immersion is practised. Parents need simply be advised to bring along the white clothes separately, so that they can be presented (just as the lighted candle is presented) after the water-bath. In the meantime, the child need only be wrapped in a blanket or shawl (a diaper also may be desirable). Where immersion is not yet possible, parents can still be directed to bring along the white robe as a change of clothes, thus preserving the original intent of the symbol: baptism is 'putting on Christ'. A change table will then be needed somewhere in or near the place of baptism.

As for older children and adult candidates, they will need direction about what to wear for the water-bath itself, and what change of clothing to provide. Some may prefer simple clothing that won't be harmed by a dunking; others may be persuaded to strip down to swim wear at the appropriate point in the ceremony. In any case, they need to wear something that can be removed easily, either before or after getting wet. The new clothes to be donned afterward may be their own and will include, preferably, something white. Alternatively, it is appropriate to provide albs for the new Christians to wear for the remainder of the day. A 'vestry' will be needed for changing out of wet clothes into the baptismal robes. This could be the regular vestry, or some improvised space with folding screens if necessary. Candidates need to be introduced to this space in advance, to satisfy themselves of its adequacy and to leave there a change of clothes (those elements of clothing that will *not* be presented in the liturgy). Obviously this space needs to be readily accessible from the worship area.

If the pool is below floor level the minister of baptism may get wet, too, at least up to the knees; and she or he will also need to change clothes. This is a situation which favours the delegation of the baptizing to an assisting presbyter or deacon, allowing the presider to remain with the congregation, without interruption for the changing of clothes.

Location of the font

How the logistics and movements within the rite work will of course depend on the location of the font/pool. There are perhaps half-a-dozen different locations commonly in use, some of which are ideal, others less so (Diagram 5):

A. At the centre-back of the worship space, usually standing inside, or just outside, the 'main' entrance.

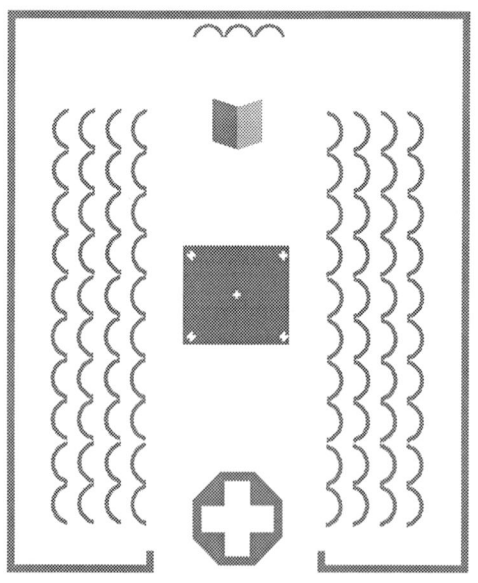

Diagram 5A.
At the centre-back of the worship space, usually standing inside, or just outside, the 'main' entrance.

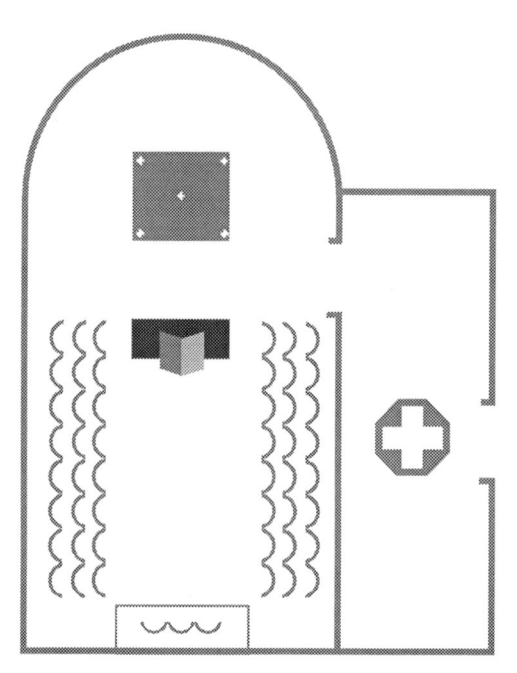

Diagram 5B.
In an adjoining area, quite outside the main worship space — whether as a separate baptistry, or in the foyer or place of preliminary assembly, where people chat before and after the liturgy.

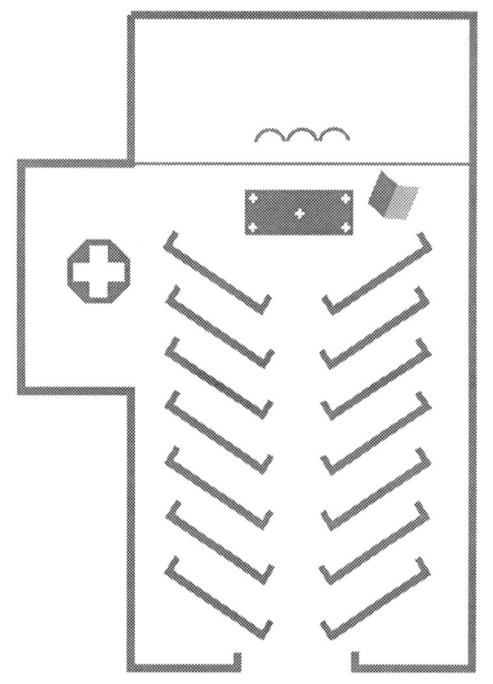

Diagram 5C.
In an alcove or baptistry off the side of the worship space.

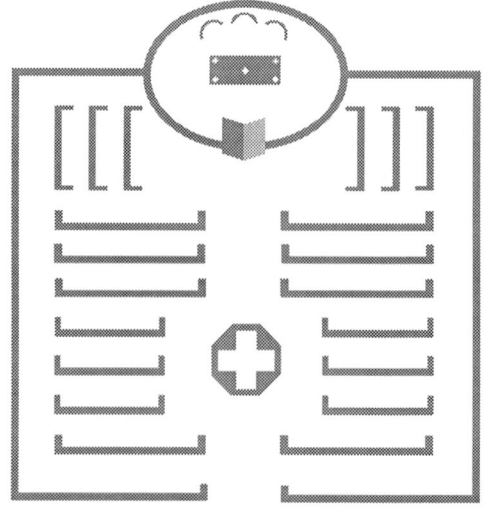

Diagram 5D.
In the midst of the congregation, sometimes with the seating around it removed to provide space for a number of folk to encircle it.

B. In an adjoining area, quite outside the main worship space — as a separate baptistry, or in the foyer or place of preliminary assembly, where people chat before and after the liturgy.

C. In an alcove or baptistry off the side of the worship space.

D. In the midst of the congregation, sometimes with the seating around it removed to provide space for a number of folk to encircle it.

E. At the front of the worship space, whether in the chancel (i.e. on the main dais) or just below it. Sometimes this will be to one side. Sometimes it will stand right in the path to the Lord's Table.

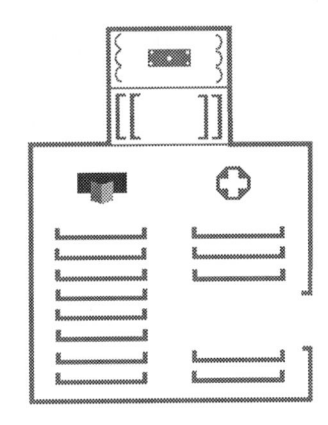

Diagram 5E.
At the front of the worship space, whether in the chancel (i.e. on the main dais), or just below it. Sometimes this will be to one side; sometimes it will stand right in the path to the Lord's Table.

There are minor improvements possible in some of these locations. It is important that a good number of people be able to encircle the font, and especially that the presider and baptismal party be able to face the congregation across the font; occasionally, a minor relocation of the font or of other furniture nearby has been helpful. But, in most cases, there are some larger issues to be faced.

We can no longer afford to ignore the fact that the purpose of the nave is to provide a place of assembly that serves (and adapts to) our needs; it is not meant to inflict upon us some inflexible 'orientation' of its own. Freedom to congregate in different configurations and to move about in the liturgy is something we need to recover. This is particularly true in baptism. In some situations we need to remove enough pews in the vicinity of the font to enable a really large crowd to gather round. It may not be possible to have the entire congregation standing around; but if the youngest are invited to come in close, and then others are encouraged to move in behind them, many more will be able to see and will feel involved; and the sense of the event will be improved for everyone, including those who still cannot see every detail of the action.

How many rooms? What must be decided first, however, is whether the worship space will be treated as one or two (or even three) rooms. We have begun to recognize the importance of this issue in relation to the eucharist; for most of us have inherited a space for worship that is really two rooms used as if they were one. In most existing church buildings the altar stands in the chancel (a room used in the middle ages for the clergy who gathered daily); but the people assemble in the nave. A common medieval custom was to bring in a nave altar when the people were assembled for the mass. Today we need to decide where the *one* altar will stand, and how it will be used. Either the altar is in the midst of the people (making the space a single room), or else the people need to process to the altar for the Celebration of the Eucharist (treating the space as two rooms). Both of these patterns have existed in Anglican places of worship; but our departure from such patterns of use has left congregations watching the action of the eucharist from afar, peering into the holy place from a place outside (and sometimes through a barrier). Slowly we are beginning to realize that this is not good enough.

So too for baptism. Whatever the configuration, we need to decide whether the baptismal space will be considered part of the nave (in which case sight lines and the reorientation of the congregation are important), or whether the baptistry will be treated as a different room, in which case it must be made large enough for the congregation to assemble there.

The question about the proper location of the font also arises when we try to provide a more adequate pool (a pool will not be migratory). Although position A, near the main entrance, has been the one frequently favoured on symbolic grounds (baptism at the entrance to 'the Church'), we need to remember that the proper candidates for baptism (of whatever age) are catechumens, not strangers. They, or their parents, need adequate experience of the Church's life before 'taking the plunge'. If baptism *is* in fact the occasion of their first introduction to the Church, it will probably be the occasion of their leaving it as well!

Some of the other options have more to commend them. Position E certainly does not, however, especially if the font is on the dais; this undermines congregational consciousness of being the baptizing community, for it supports the illusion that liturgy is what the ministers do 'on stage' for the benefit of an 'audience'. It may result in a trivialization of the font as well.

Whether people can see the action at the font (wherever it may be situated) is usually more a matter of where they are standing at that moment. Baptisms are good occasions for transcending the rigid boundaries which pews impose on us. The creation of a baptistry as a separate room is worth considering, provided it is large enough for the congregation to assemble there.

Wherever it be placed, the font/pool should have enough space around it to allow ministers and baptism party to assemble there without crowding. There should be room for an ample shelf or table to hold all things necessary for the ceremony; an aumbry for chrism may also be desirable in this location; and a change table for the infant candidates will frequently be required in the vicinity.

Mass baptism in the Volga River, July 1991.

PREPARING FOR THE LITURGY

The preparation of candidates (or their parents) for baptism is a subject beyond the scope of this manual; see the resources for developing the catechumenate, listed in Appendix 1. Suffice it to say that it is the baptismal rite itself which implies the *minimum* scope of such preparation. With the support of the Christian community, candidates deserve the opportunity to discover (a) what it is they really seek from God, (b) whether the baptismal covenant is indeed the covenant into which they believe they are called, and (c) what are the evils they must renounce to follow Christ. They need an actual experience of sharing in the life of the community of faith where these issues are addressed. Simply being asked these questions 'out of the blue' on the day of their baptism means nothing whatsoever.

Preparing the candidates

Sponsors need preparation too. They need to know exactly what their responsibilities are, and they need adequate opportunity to get to know the candidates and what the candidates intend by baptism. For most of us, the ministry of sponsors is a whole new field to be explored. (Resources for this are listed in Appendix 1.)

The more immediate preparation of sponsors is done in rehearsal. Those who are being baptized (or their parents if they are young children) may be helped by rehearsal, if only to resolve anxieties about what will really happen. But they need not become experts in ritual choreography; indeed there is a real peril that they

Preparing the sponsors

could become so preoccupied with doing the right thing that they could fail to experience the ritual as a moment of grace. For this reason it is better that their preparation focus on the meaning of the covenant they are to enter, the threshold they are to cross. It is the sponsors above all who need to be rehearsed in the ritual movements; then they can guide the candidates (or their parents) through the ceremony. Alternatively, a **master of baptismal ceremonies** may be assigned to direct these movements. Rehearsals for candidates (or parents of candidates) have too often become a substitute for real baptismal preparation.

Adult candidates and parents of child candidates do need, however, an opportunity *after the event* to reflect on the meaning of what they have experienced, and to cultivate their consciousness of these signs as the clues to this new existence. It is important to inform the baptismal party early of plans for post-baptismal formation as a clear signal that baptism is not something you 'get done', but a new beginning.

Preparing the readers

The Additional Directions on page 163 of the BAS remind us of the importance of preparing readers, and suggest that this is a role sponsors may play. If they do, rehearsal of the readings can be combined with rehearsal of the ritual. This of course presupposes that the sponsors are suitable candidates for reading on other grounds as well; no symbolic advantage can outweigh the offence given by readings which cannot be heard, or of readers who cannot make clear that they understand and care about what they are reading.

Preparing the community

The baptizing community deserves an opportunity to prepare as well. At the very least the faithful need to know in advance not only the baptismal days, but who the candidates are;

they need to be assured that these candidates are genuine in their quest; and their responsibility as the baptizing community needs to be honoured by including the candidates in the Prayers of the People. One way to help in this is to have the first part of the Presentation and Examination (i.e., the action detailed on page 153 of the BAS) take place at an earlier service some weeks before the day of the baptism. (A more substantial form of this proposal may be found in *Making Disciples*, pp. 32-35.)

Finally, all the chief ministers in the liturgy, including presbyters, require preparation. Sometimes baptismal celebrations give the impression that because they are occasional, they are necessarily casual — unrehearsed, awkward, full of unpremeditated minor crises, and punctuated by ad hoc explanations. Baptismal liturgy ought to be marked by the same care and confidence and the same powerful dignity that we expect in all great and solemn celebrations. Movements need to be planned in advance, and carefully rehearsed with servers and other liturgical ministers. The musicians also need to have a sure grasp of the movement of the rite, and of the precise role that will be played by the music.

Preparing the ministers

The bishop, when presiding, will need to be briefed in advance, though this may be only in writing. An annotated copy of the rite, indicating the intended movements is helpful. In particular, a bishop who has not presided at a baptism involving immersion may appreciate some procedural suggestions when immersion and a more generous annointing with chrism are planned.

The part of bishop's chaplain, however, may be taken by a member of the local community — a server, perhaps; and this person will certainly be included in the rehearsal.

Preparing the bishop

Preparing the room In addition to preparing people, the room and the materials for the celebration must be prepared:
- water (the pool, if there is one, must be filled in advance and the temperature adjusted)
- a pitcher or ewer of water (to pour into the font/pool before the Thanksgiving over the Water, unless there is running water in the pool already)
- a pitcher or cruet of oil (and perhaps a basin of soapy water and a towel for washing oil off the presider's hands after the anointing),
- towels (an ample supply of large hotel-style white towels is ideal)
- candles for presentation
- new clothes for presentation
- a vestry for the candidates to change in
- a change table for infants
- reserved places in the room for the baptismal party
- books and leaflets for the baptismal party
- seating for the bishop and the bishop's chaplain (normally the bishop takes the seat reserved for the presider), and
- the paschal candle lit.

If a temporary (larger) font or pool is planned, it should be installed well in advance, and experimented with. If it is the custom to sprinkle the congregation after the baptism, some implement for this (possibly an evergreen bough or leafy branch) must be provided. The paschal candle is always lit for baptisms; and outside of the Easter season it stands near the font/pool.

The liturgical colour is normally that of the day. If the presider is to wear a chasuble for the celebration of the eucharist, it will of course be worn for the baptism as well.

Reception It is good to have a reception after the service. Many parents of infant candidates plan family receptions of their own to follow the celebration; and it is important for parish sponsors to attend these parties if possible. But it is even more important that the congregation assert *its* place as the new household of the baptized, and insist that the congregational reception take precedence over any private parties. This, of course, must be explained to families well in advance, so that they can plan the timing of the domestic party which may still follow.

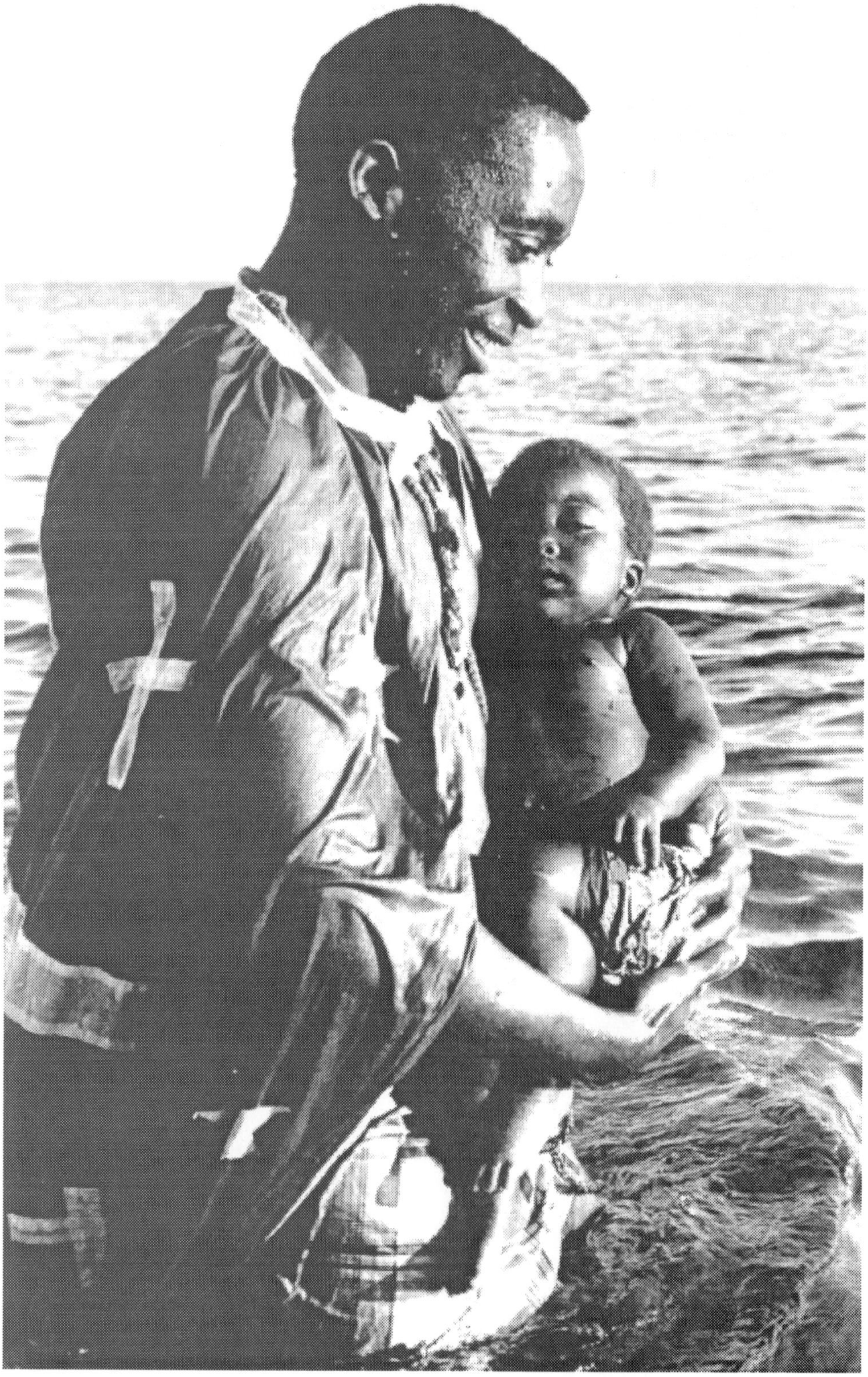

CELEBRATING THE LITURGY

Notes offered here presuppose a careful reading of the BAS order for Holy Baptism, including the notes Concerning the Service (page 150) and the Additional Directions (page 163-64). Many options and alternatives will be mentioned in what follows—not to suggest perpetual variation and experiment, but to invite communities to think through in detail all aspects of the ceremony in the light of local physical arrangements and local custom, and then to decide on what seems the most faithful pattern of celebration.

The integration of baptism into the Great Vigil of Easter is outside the scope of this manual, and will be treated in a subsequent publication in this series. On any other occasion, the rite has this basic shape:

The Gathering of the Community: This is the time for greeting, and recalling the faith in which we gather; and it culminates in prayer. Gathering has a special character and importance on these occasions because baptisms often bring together numerous visitors, some of whom are strangers to our ways and must be acknowledged, welcomed, and incorporated.

The Proclamation of the Word: This consists of scripture readings, psalmody, anthems, hymns, and preaching. The sermon provides an opportunity to make sense of our practice of scheduling baptisms at the great festive moments in the Church's life: the sermon must do justice to the festival; but at the same time it can lead people to see the new light cast upon baptism by the particular festival, and *vice versa*.

The Presentation and Examination of the Candidates: Candidates (or their parents) are invited to declare publicly their intentions; then they turn from the ways of evil and give themselves to Christ; and the community pledges its support for them. As a transition to the next act, all join in solemn prayer for the candidates. This is the drama of conversion, the human side of the initiation, in response to the word proclaimed; and it leads us into

The Celebration of Baptism: We offer thanks over the water, remembering the story of salvation; the candidates are sworn into the baptismal covenant, while all the baptized join with them, reaffirming their own baptism into this covenant; and then the candidates go down into the water. Coming up, they are marked with the sign of the anointed one, clothed anew, acknowledged as fellow members before God, and welcomed into the body of disciples. They are greeted with the sign of our reconciliation, the kiss of peace. This is the drama of death and resurrection, of self-surrender and union in love. This new relationship is consummated in

The Celebration of the Eucharist: The new Christians immediately share in the royal priesthood of the baptized as they present the gifts at the Table; then together we offer thanks for this new covenant, sealed in the blood of Christ; we break bread and feed on Christ and are dismissed, that we may be Christ for the world.

The gathering, and the proclamation of the Word

In more detail, the shape unfolds in the following way: before the service begins the baptismal party may be seated in places reserved for them in the midst of the congregation; or they may be included in the entrance procession and thus led to the place reserved for them. Candidates for confirmation/reception/reaffirmation (if there are any) may be seated with them. The rite begins much as other celebrations of the eucharist do (see *Let Us Give Thanks* for guidance on the Gathering and Proclamation).

The readings are those appointed for the day. The possible exception to this rule is the occasion of a 'baptismal festival', and only during ordinary time; this commonly happens because the bishop is not available on any of the designated festivals. On such an occasion, one or more of the readings listed on page 165 may be appropriate, although resorting to this table of lessons disrupts the integrity of the regular Proclamation of the Word, as provided in the Sunday lectionary. The proper lections need to be retained during Advent and Eastertide. (During Lent, baptisms will be postponed till Easter, anyway! See Appendix 7.)

How long is the ceremony?

To some, this rite becomes a marathon — two sacraments, twice the time! This is not quite true; nevertheless we might reasonably expect those acts which are central and constitutive of the Christian life to take time. However, if we plan and rehearse carefully, and take full advantage of the opportunities provided for compression, the service need not be much longer than a celebration of the eucharist. The Nicene Creed is left out (we declare our faith in the baptismal creed); the Prayers of the People may be omitted (intercessions can still be included in the eucharistic prayer: see Appendix 3); and the confession and absolution are omitted, for we celebrate our reconciliation as we renew our own baptismal covenant and exchange the Peace. More than this, it is possible to relocate the first part of the Presentation (page 153) to an earlier occasion (see the comments under Preparing for the Liturgy, page 29); the movement to the font can, in some settings take place during the Prayers for the Candidates; if there are many candidates, two or more baptizers can coordinate their actions to keep that part of the rite from being too prolonged; the Giving of the Light can be shortened with the help of many hands and take place simultaneously for all the new Christians. The ceremonies following the water-bath (including the exchange of the Peace) can, in some configurations, all take place beside the font, eliminating the movement to the front of the room (see the comments on page 48).

The presentation and examination of the candidates

Location of the presentation and examination

The location used for the renunciations and act of adherence, which culminate this next part of the rite, depends on whether this is truly an act, or merely words. In the text there is a sudden and surprising eruption of talk about Satan, powers of evil, and sinful desires. This strains the credulity of the secular mind, which has become flaccid in face of the evils of our time. But the practice of the ancient Church grounded these provocative references in a clear and very physical sense of what is really taking place. Candidates stood at the door, on the edge of the assembly; they faced outward as they made their renunciation of evil (sometimes they were even asked to spit in that direction); then they would turn toward the assembly as they spoke of turning to Christ. This was especially powerful in the context of the Great Vigil: outside was darkness, into which they spoke as they renounced the *powers* of darkness; inside was the light of Christ, rising in glory, toward which they turned. In this act, then, they dramatically broke off all allegiance or obligation to the old master, turned their back upon the evil one, and gave themselves into the service of Christ. Whenever this is done today, it reveals its meaning to participants in a way that words alone can hardly do; and it is not quickly forgotten (Diagram 6).

To do this requires only that the Presentation, the renunciations, and the act of adherence take place just inside one of the principal entrances to the room (it need not be the 'west' door, although 'west' certainly has symbolic significance). After the sermon, the presider moves to that door to meet the baptismal party, preceded by the server(s) who will assist in the baptism, other presbyters or deacons who will assist in baptizing, and possibly a cantor. A deacon or server may lead, bearing the lighted paschal candle, if it is the Easter season. A server may carry the Presider's book. At the same time, one of the sponsors (who has rehearsed this), or the master of baptismal ceremonies, leads the baptismal party to the door (preferably by a different route than the presider takes to get there, so that they meet at the spot).

The bishop, if present, presides at the baptism, and proceeds to the place of the presentations, carrying the staff. The mitre may also be worn. Staff and mitre need not be relinquished until the bishop is standing at the font.

Before the presider begins to move to the location of the presentations, however, the congregation may be invited to stand. This is helpful, particularly if they all must turn around in order to see the action, impossible to do while sitting. The baptismal party should be entirely in place by the time the presider and other ministers arrive; then the presider begins with the words, "The candidate...will now be presented" (or other suitable introduction if the Presentation has already occurred on an earlier occasion).

One very practical contribution that a sponsor can make is to hold the book for a candidate (or their parents), ensuring that the candidate always knows the place and does not have to carry a book during the successive moments of the ceremony.

Presentation Note that adults are presented first; as each is presented, he or she is asked, "Do you desire to be baptized?" By contrast, when the children are presented, the questions that follow must wait till all the children have been presented; the questions are then asked of all the parents and other sponsors as a group.

Diagram 6.

Turning Before proceeding to the question, "Do you renounce Satan...?" the presider may wait for the entire party to turn and face out the door (which must be open at this point!). A whispered reminder may be needed. The appropriate gesture for the act of renunciation is one or both arms thrust forward with hands up, palms out, a gesture of resistance. The sponsors may need to model this posture. Before beginning the fourth question, the presider may wait for the party to begin turning back toward the congregation. As they turn, they are asked, "Do you turn to Christ...?"

The notes on page 163 of the BAS imply that this action could, if necessary, take place at the font. However, it is worth finding an alternative to this, in order to make clear the distinctiveness of these very different actions, and to avoid the impression that baptism is an endless string of wordy questions and answers. In some configurations, the Presentation and Examination may need to take place at the front of the room; in this case, it is better for the baptismal party to face the congregation, and for the presider, with back to the congregation, to face them. The questions, after all, are asked on behalf of the baptizing community, and it is they who need to hear the answers.

If there are candidates for confirmation, reception, or reaffirmation, they may now be called to step forward (simply by the bishop's announcement to the congregation, "The other candidates will now be presented"). The members of the baptismal party may remain where they are; the other candidates move into the middle of the congregation, and answer from there.

Reafirmation candidates

Finally, the presider asks the community to declare its support for all the candidates. This, too, requires the presider to turn from the candidates to face the congregation directly.

The Prayers for the Candidates which follow presuppose the *human* action (the renunciations and act of adherence), and anticipate the *divine* action that follows (the celebration of baptism). Our prayers express our hope for all that God will do for these candidates in the baptismal

Procession to the font

waters. To begin to move toward the font at this point helps make clear this inner movement of hope. It is difficult to imagine a configuration in which the distance of this procession would be too short to be worth the trouble. Candidates for confirmation, reception, or reaffirmation need to be drawn into this procession as well, as it moves through the congregation. Someone other than the presider leads the litany; it can be a deacon or someone else who represents the community, or it can be one of the sponsors.

It is quite appropriate to sing this litany, and the cantor can be part of the procession to the font. The party should arrive at the font by the time the litany is ending. If the procession lasts longer than this, it may be accompanied by the singing of a psalm (for example, psalm 42), and the Prayers for the Candidates may be offered upon arrival at the font. (See Appendix 2 for musical settings.)

Diagram 7

The procession might include some or all of the following:

- a deacon or server bearing the paschal candle (especially during the Easter season, when the candle normally stands near the altar or lectern, and needs to be moved to the font for the baptism);
- the crucifer;
- the cantor;
- the master of baptismal ceremonies;
- sponsors leading their candidates;
- servers who will assist at the font;
- other deacons, and the presbyter(s);

- the presider (who may be the bishop).

If the baptistry is a separate room, the procession will also include the entire congregation following the candidates, and followed in turn by the servers, presbyters, and bishop. If the baptistry will be crowded, the congregation may have to *follow* the bishop or presbyter, just to ensure that the latter actually reaches the font!

The celebration of baptism
Before the Thanksgiving over the Water begins, it is appropriate that people be invited to gather around the water (and those who are very small be brought to the front so that they can see). Newborn Christians are drawn out of the waters of the womb of mother Church; and a sense of the enclosing community is most fitting at this moment. The presider stands facing the people across the water.

Candidates for confirmation/reception/reaffirmation are properly included in the party which clusters around the font or pool. The water is an important sign for them, too, as they reaffirm their baptismal faith.

This is the moment for pouring water into the font/pool, unless the pool already has water running into it. If the font is large enough to be worthy of the name, the addition may be only a token; but the sound of running water at this point is important. Therefore the gesture needs to be bold — a noisy splashing, from a considerable height. This may be done by a server; or, if the pool is low enough, it may be done by one of the children gathered around.

If the presider is going to administer the baptism as well, and if the pool is large enough to permit the baptizer to enter with the candidates, this is the moment for the presider to remove shoes and step into the water.

Thanksgiving over the water

Now the presider offers the Prayer of Thanksgiving; and it is fitting that it be sung (see the comments on singing in *Let Us Give Thanks*, page 37). Although this prayer stands in a different relation to the sacrament than does the Great Thanksgiving to the eucharist (only in the eucharist is the thanksgiving essential to the 'form' of the sacrament), nevertheless, as a solemn thanksgiving in its own right, the prayer should be offered with the same dignity. If possible, a server can hold the book so that the presider may assume the classical posture, hands open and outstretched. At the words, "Now sanctify this water...", the paschal candle may be dipped into the water, as was done at the Great Vigil of Easter (Diagram 8).

Diagram 8

It is appropriate that the congregation stand for this act of thanksgiving, and for all that follows, up to and including the prayer, "Heavenly Father, we thank you that by water and the Holy Spirit..." (BAS, page 160).

The BAS provides two forms of the Thanksgiving over the Water. Note that in the first form, in the fifth paragraph, the presider is expected to name the candidate(s); a list of names may be inserted into the presider's book.

The Baptismal Covenant

Then follows the Baptismal Covenant. The triune God is proclaimed not only in the formula said as water is administered, but in the even more substantial proclamation of the baptismal creed. This communal profession of faith has been restored, in the BAS, to its rightful place immediately before the descent into the water; its origins are in the profession of faith made during the baptismal action itself. Candidates who must partially disrobe to enter the water can do so at this point, *before* the Baptismal Covenant, rather than immediately before entering the water; in this way, the unity of profession-of-faith and immersion-in-water can be maintained.

The great questions of the baptismal covenant must be asked not only of the baptismal party but of the whole congregation; and the presider may take a position that expresses this. The bishop, if present, takes back the staff and, if desired, the mitre, before asking the questions; the bishop may keep staff and mitre through the administration of baptism, if someone else is administering.

The water bath

Then the first candidate is brought (or carried) to the water. The baptizer may choose at this point to roll up one or both sleeves, perhaps with the help of a server. (If long-sleeved streetclothes are worn underneath, these sleeves can be rolled up before the service, when vesting.) It may be hoped that the baptizer already knows the candidate's name and does not need to ask;

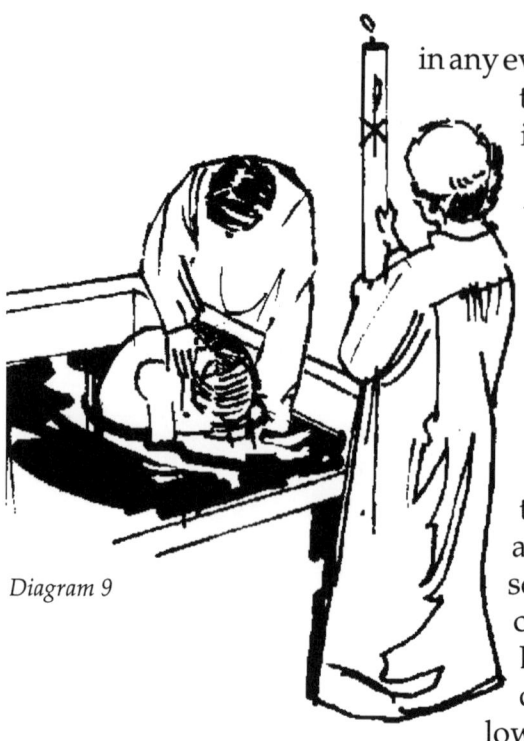

in any event, asking the name is not meant to be audible to the community, as if this were a naming ceremony.

When an adult or older child is to be immersed, the sponsors may assist the candidate in stepping into the water. The candidate may kneel and the one baptizing places one hand on the back of the candidate's neck and the other on the candidate's forehead, pushing head and shoulders down into the water and lifting the head up again three times; or water may be scooped up and poured over the candidate's head three times (see Diagram 9). Alternatively, the candidate may sit in the water and be lowered backward into a reclining position three times, with the baptizer's arm behind the candidate's shoulders.

Diagram 9

For a young child or infant, the level of the water largely determines the way the baptizer will proceed: if the water level is below the level of the baptizer's knees, bending over to dip the candidate can be back-breaking; kneeling beside or in the water may be necessary. An infant may be held with its head at the baptizer's elbow, and the forearm under its back, hand gripping one thigh; the other hand may be on top to protect its nose. If a child's head is not to be completely under water, one arm may be placed under the back, with the hand gripping the far arm, and the other arm under the buttocks, hand gripping the far leg. The child may then be lowered into the water three times. During the threefold immersion (note that the rubrics call for *im*mersion rather than *sub*mersion), the baptizer recites the baptismal formula (Diagram 10).

If the font is too small for immersion of the

Diagram 10

Diagram 11

candidate, it is sufficient to stand the candidate in a catch-basin beside it, or to hold the candidate's head over the font, and pour water over the head. Note that the goal here is *not* to save the candidate's coiffure or composure. This is the sacrament of death and resurrection, of new birth, of spiritual washing, of life arising out of watery chaos; and none of these images will justify the timidity of our conventional behaviour in baptism (which seems to do little more than reassure everyone that there is nothing here to be alarmed about!). Water should be used liberally and noisily. If the floor ends up flooded, that is not the fault of the baptizer, but of the inadequate facilities. Again, we must not allow the building or its furnishings to compromise our central symbols. If the baptismal towels owned by the parish are the size of handkerchiefs, they will have to be dedicated to some

Diagram 12

INTO THE HOUSEHOLD OF GOD   45

more dainty purpose, and replaced by proper bath towels (Diagrams 11 and 12).

Decency   This fullness of symbolism has implications for more than hairdos; when we restore the normative use of water, questions will inevitably be raised about decency and decorum. There are some things we can do to respect current sensibilities (although people frequently encounter near nudity in public in this culture). If adult candidates or older children want to wear more than swim suits, it should be something dark in colour. And there is nothing wrong with infants wearing diapers into the water, if it saves the parents and subsequent candidates misgivings about the cleanliness of the water. But we dare not try too hard to preserve decorum, or we will end up domesticating this awesome sign. Birth is primitive, natural, and profoundly intimate. This is the moment when the personal and public interests intersect at the deepest level.

The signing   The signing, which may be accompanied by anointing with chrism, is intended to follow each baptism, rather than waiting till all candidates have come up from the water. Candidates who have been immersed are signed (and anointed) before leaving the water. Although chrismation should not upstage the water-bath (it is an explanatory gesture), it ought to be more than a greasy smear. Conventional oil-stocks conceal the fact that oil is being used; a cruet or pitcher of oil is more eloquent. Once again, daintiness can become the enemy of symbolic gesture. What is intended here is a sacramental announcement that this new Christian shares in the anointing of the Christ, and is now a member of the royal priesthood. Chrism is customarily scented with oil of balsam or some other fragrant oil (such as may be obtained from an Orthodox supply shop or a supplier of bath

Diagram 13

oils). It is this scent which gives substance to the metaphor of the 'sweet fragrance of Christ', a fragrance that lingers wherever the newly baptized go. Thus, it is appropriate to pour oil on the head, or on the forehead with the head tipped back; the sign of the cross can then be marked in the oil on the forehead (Diagrams 13-15). Alternatively, a server may pour oil into the presider's palm, who then spreads it over the new Christian's forehead, and marks in the oil the sign of the cross. The oil may be massaged down the face and neck and onto the torso as well, to make the gesture more generous. Once all candidates have been baptized and anointed a server brings a basin of soapy water and a towel for the presider.

Note that the *presider* is the minister of this signing (and chrismation), and says the prayer following, even if the immersion has been delegated to an assisting presbyter or deacon. If the bishop is presiding, the mitre might be worn for the signing (and chrismation), but it is removed for the prayer that follows.

When an infant or young child has been baptized and signed, and then wrapped in a towel, it is appropriate that the child be handed to a parish sponsor, signifying the adoption of the child into the new household of faith. The child's eventual return to its parents recalls the rever-

Diagram 14   *Diagram 15*

ent guardianship seen in the parents of Jesus himself.

The prayer over the new Christians

The prayer that follows is to be said with hands outstretched over (or towards) all the new Christians together, and "at a place in full sight of the congregation". The note on page 164 of the BAS amplifies this rubric, suggesting a return to the front of the room. The point of this is that the newly baptized have now emerged from the 'liminal' place of baptism into the full assembly of the faithful. This is especially important if the location of the baptism is such that the congregation has been cut off from the action. But if the faithful are in fact all gathered around the font/pool, this relocation is not necessary and everything up to and including the sign of Peace can take place there. Indeed, even the laying-on-of-hands for confirmation/reception/ reaffirmation can take place beside the font. More of that later.

The giving of the light and the new clothes

If no relocation to the front of the room is required, the BAS order actually works better; for if the paschal candle stands beside the font, it is unnatural to move very far away before taking light from the candle for the Giving of the Light. If new clothes are to be given, this takes place immediately following the gift of light (see Appendix 4 for a suggested form of words).

The new clothes are presented to an infant simply by draping the clothes over the child. One of the parents may take the child to a change table after the welcome.

The presentation of gifts — the light, the new clothes, etc. — may be done by appointed representatives of the community. This is an ideal role for children, no matter what the ages of the candidates. Each candle is lit from the paschal candle and then handed to the new Christian (or to a parent or sponsor of a young child). These

Diagram 16

presentations can be made to all the newly baptized simultaneously simply by recruiting enough help from the congregation.

Then follows the welcome. After this the newly baptized may be helped into an alb, or sent off to change (before the Peace); the one who administered baptism may also need to change at this point. Songs or psalms may be sung while the congregation waits for their return. Psalm 23 is particularly fitting here; or repeated chants, such as those of Taizé, can provide both a meditative exercise and an interval of whatever length may be needed. (See Appendix 2, vesting hymns, for further suggestions.)

Another element appropriately included in a baptismal celebration is some use of the water

Water for the congregation

Diagram 17

as a sign of the congregation's renewal in the baptismal covenant. This may take the form of *asperges* or sprinkling: the presider or an assistant can dip an evergreen bough or leafy branch into the water and sprinkle the assembly. Or better still, there can be a congregational procession past the water, giving everyone a chance to touch the water and mark themselves with the sign of the cross, or to use whatever gesture they wish to reaffirm their baptismal identity. For children who have been eager to feel the water themselves, this is a wonderful opportunity to do so in a significant way. For adults, such an opportunity to take initiative in this tangible sign of renewal makes it preferable to the more passive (and inescapable) participation in a sprinkling. If a hymn is used while waiting for new Christians to change into new clothes, this provides an excellent time for either of these gestures. (Alternatively, if the baptismal party processes to a place before the congregation for the prayer "Heavenly Father, we thank you that by water and the Holy Spirit...", sprinkling may occur during this brief movement.)

Reaffirmation

If there are candidates for confirmation/reception/reaffirmation, they will be prayed for with the laying-on-of-hands, following the welcome of the newly baptized. This can take place right beside the font, the candidates standing to receive this ministration. No posture is specified for the bishop in the laying-on-of-hands-with-prayer; however, the bishop is *required* to stand for the laying-on-of-hands-with-prayer in ordination; this is the normal posture for such a ministration. It is entirely appropriate, then, for the bishop to stand next to the font for affirmation of the Baptismal Covenant (Diagram 17). This also reduces the danger that confirmation might once again upstage baptism (a danger most apparent when the bishop returns to the centre and sits on a 'throne' for the laying-on-of-hands!).

The bishop does not wear the mitre during the laying-on-of-hands in prayer. After the invitation to the whole congregation to pray, a period of silence is kept. The congregation may be invited to remain standing. The bishop says the appointed prayer with hands outstretched over all the candidates; then the bishop goes to each of them in succession. Sponsors need to be ready to name each of the candidates for the bishop. After all have been prayed for individually, the bishop again prays for them as a group with hands outstretched; for this reason, the newly reaffirmed must remain standing before the bishop (rather than returning to their places as soon as hands have been laid on them).

Any attempt to present *the newly baptized* to the bishop for confirmation is entirely redundant, and a complete violation of the integrity of the rite. (See the report of the Confirmation Taskforce, listed in Appendix 1.)

The Peace   The sign of Peace concludes this part of the baptismal sequence. This is above all a sign of reconciliation. Baptism itself is the fundamental sacrament of reconciliation with God and with one another in Christ; and the Peace makes this aspect explicit. It is important that the presider, after offering this sign to all in the general greeting, go first to greet the new Christians and offer a truly generous sign of welcome. Others can then follow, and may be helped to do so by explicit invitation. It is at this moment that all the pent-up anticipation, nervousness, gratitude, and wonder can break through in a communal sign of joy and affirmation. If there is a way for the newly baptized to remain in the open (rather than returning to a pew) during this greeting, it will be much easier to give full expression to this gesture. For example, if there were also candidates for the laying-on-of-hands to come to the bishop before the Peace, there is no reason to dismiss the baptismal party from the scene during that action. They would remain standing nearby during the laying-on-of-hands; and then they and those who have reaffirmed the covenant could be greeted together in the Peace.

Intercessions   It is desirable to include intercessions in the baptismal liturgy. One method is to include timely intercessions in the eucharistic prayer (as in prayer 6, BAS page 210). Another is to offer intercessions *after*, rather than *before*, the Peace. The Peace is kept adjacent to the baptismal rite itself as the first acknowledgement of the reconciliation won in baptism. Prayers of the People after the Peace provide a sign of the nature of the priestly community into which new Christians have been initiated; but such prayers need to be especially concise and appropriate to this occasion. (See Appendix 3 for models.) It is *not* appropriate to include the general confession and absolution; the supreme sacrament of reconciliation has just been celebrated!

Following the exchange of the Peace, members of the baptismal party may be conducted to their place in the congregation; and the presider and other ministers return to their places, too. If the procession of gifts for the eucharist follows immediately, those who will carry the gifts go instead to the place where the gifts are waiting. Again, a sponsor, or the master of baptismal ceremonies, may need to accompany them and direct this action.

The celebration of the eucharist

Now follows the Preparation of the Gifts; and all the new Christians (or at least all the adults and older children) can be involved in the procession of gifts to the Holy Table, as the note in BAS page 164 suggests. One of them may carry a baptismal candle in this procession and light the candles at the altar. These roles are eloquent signs that the new Christians share with us in the royal priesthood of Christ; and it is appropriate to keep them involved in this service, perhaps on a rotating basis, throughout the Sundays following their baptism.

The preparation of the gifts

During the procession of gifts a hymn is usually sung; and in some settings the entire congregation will join in this procession in order to gather around the Table of the Lord and offer thanksgiving. If the baptism took place in a separate room, then it is during this hymn that the members if the congregation will process back to their places, or gather around the altar.

For further guidance with this part of the liturgy, see *Let Us Give Thanks*.

Communion of the newly baptized

One detail of Holy Communion deserves comment here: it must be made clear that baptism is consummated in communion. All the newly baptized need to be directed to come and share in the sacrament of this communion on the day of their baptism. (The BAS does not even tell us how to combine baptism with Morning or Evening Prayer, because there is no reason to try.) Even infants share at the Lord's Table: a drop of wine is placed in an infant's mouth, either with a finger-tip dipped in the cup, or with a spoon; the parents may appropriately be involved in administering communion in this way.

In some parishes, infant communion may still be a novelty. If parents are not anticipating this, they need to be instructed in advance. It is hardly fair to offer this as an option, as if it were up to them to judge whether it is really appropriate. They simply need to be told that this is the traditional practice and shown how it will take place.

Thus unfolds the great drama of our salvation. Baptized into the death of the Lord, raised up to share his eternal priesthood, we are welcomed into the divine communion, the very household of God.

Appendix 1: RESOURCES

Developing the Catechumenate

Catechumenate: a Journal of Christian Initiation. Chicago: Liturgy Training Publications; published six times a year. *Brings together some of the best Roman Catholic experience and thinking.*

Hill, John W. B. **Making Disciples.** Toronto: Hoskin Books, 1991. *A proposal for the restoration of the catechumenate, based on the rites of the Book of Alternative Services.*

Holeton, David, ed. **Growing in Newness of Life.** Toronto: Anglican Book Centre, 1993. *The preparatory essays for the Fourth International Anglican Liturgical Consultation (Toronto, 1991). See especially the essay by Philip May on baptismal symbolism, and an essay by John Hill and Paul Bowie on the Catechuminate. The book includes as an appendix the concluding statement of the consultation, which is also published separately: see next item.*

_____, **Christian Initiation in the Anglican Communion.** Bramcote: Grove Books, 1991. *The statement of the Fourth International Anglican Liturgical Consultation (Toronto, 1991), 'Walk in Newness of Life'; a careful reconsideration of initiation, including recommendations on the catechumenate.*

Keifert, Patrick R. **Welcoming the Stranger.** Minneapolis: The Fortress Press, 1992. *A Lutheran exposition of the nature of public ritual and how people are initiated into it; timely observations about the need for both the public and the intimate in Christian formation.*

Merriman, Michael, ed. **The Baptismal Mystery and the Catechumenate.** New York: Church Hymnal Corporation, 1990. *Papers presented at the first Episcopal Church conference on the catechumenate.*

The Catechumenal Process: Adult Initiation and Formation for Christian Ministry. New York: Church Hymnal Corporation, 1990. *A practical guide to help dioceses and congregations develop appropriate patterns of preparation for baptism and the renewal of the baptismal life.*

The Catechumenate: Formation for Church Membership. Alexandria, Virginia: Associated Parishes, 1991. *A brief exposition of the ministry of basic formation based on the rites of the (Episcopal) Book of Occasional Services, 2nd edition.*

The Ministry of Sponsors

Hill, John W. B. **Making Disciples.** Toronto: Hoskin Books, 1991. *See chapter 4.*

Lewinski, Ron. **Guide for Sponsors.** Chicago: Liturgy Training Publications, 1987. *A comprehensive treatment from a Roman Catholic perspective.*

Wilde, James A., ed. **Finding and Forming Sponsors and Godparents.** Chicago: Liturgy Training Publications, 1988. *Essays covering a wide range of issues, many of which could be translated into an Anglican context.*

Baptismal Space

Davies, J. G. **The Architectural Setting of Baptism.** London: Barrie and Rockliff, 1962. *An historical study.*

Huffman, Walter C., and S. Anita Stauffer. **Where We Worship.** Minneapolis: Augsburg Publishing, 1987. *A well-illustrated congregational guide for rethinking liturgical space; there is also a leaders' guide of the same title.*

Kuehn, Regina. **A Place for Baptism.** Chicago: Liturgy Training Publications, 1992. *Kuehn is a photographer as well as a liturgical consultant, and portrays some of the best design work in U.S. catholicism.*

Dressing the Church, Liturgy, Volume 5, Number 4. The Liturgical Conference, 1986. *See especially the articles, S. Anita Stauffer* A Place for Burial Birth and Bath; *and James Notebaart* The Font and the Assembly.

Mauck, Marchita. **Shaping a House for the Church.** Chicago: Liturgy Training Publications, 1990. *A well illustrated introduction to the challenges of liturgical architecture.*

National Conference of Catholic Bishops. **Environment and Art in Catholic Worship.** Chicago: Liturgy Training Publications, 1986. *One of the most lucid statements of the principles of liturgical architecture and furnishing.*

Stauffer, S. Anita. **Re-examining Baptismal Fonts: Baptismal Spaces for the Contemporary Church.** (Videotape) Collegeville: The Liturgical Press, 1991. *An examination of fonts past and present with commentary.*

White, James F., and Susan J. White. **Church Architecture: Building and Renovating for Christian Worship.** Nashville: Abingdon Press, 1988. *See especially the chapter on 'A Place for Baptism'.*

Celebrating Baptism and Eucharist

Buchanan, Colin O. **Adult Baptisms.** Bramcote: Grove Books, 1985. *Principles and practice; based on the (Church of England) Alternative Services Book.*

Associated Parishes, Alexandria, Virginia: 1987. *A brief pamphlet designed for the general reader; based on the 1979 (Episcopal) Book of Common Prayer.*

Eastman, A. Theodore. **The Baptizing Community: Christian Initiation and the Local Community.** Harrisburg: Morehouse Publishing; revised edition, 1991. *Historical and pastoral principles for restoring baptism to its proper place in the life of the Church; based on the rites of the 1979 (Episcopal) Book of Common Prayer. Includes models and examples.*

Galley, Howard E. **The Ceremonies of the Eucharist: A Guide to Celebration.** Cambridge, Mass: Cowley Publications, 1989. *A guide to the use of the rites of the 1979 (Episcopal) Book of Common Prayer; it includes sections on 'the Holy Eucharist with Baptism', and 'The Bishop at Holy Baptism'.*

Holeton, David, Catherine Hall, and Gregory Kerr-Wilson. **Let Us Give Thanks.** Toronto: Hoskin Books, 1991. *A guide for celebrating the eucharist according to the Book of Alternative Services.*

Ross, Robert, **Preparing for Baptism.** Toronto: The Anglican Book Centre, *1993. A very accessible exposition of the BAS rite of baptism, with questions for reflection and discussion at the end of each section.*

Young Children and the Eucharist

Buchanan, Colin, ed. **Nurturing Children in Communion.** Bramcote: Grove Books, 1985. *Preparatory essays for the First (Boston) Anglican Liturgical Consultation (1985), from which issued the Boston Statement on Children and Communion (included as an appendix).*

Holeton, David. **Infant Communion—Then and Now.** Bramcote: Grove Books, 1981. *A fascinating story of the way this practice has shaped ecclesial consciousness in the past.*

_____, "Communion of All the Baptized and Anglican Tradition", **Anglican Theological Review** 69, 1 (1987) pp 13-28.

Müller-Fahrenholz, Geiko, ed. **...and do not hinder them.** [Faith and Order paper 109] Geneva, 1982.

Appendix 2: MUSIC

Music within the celebration of baptism can be a problem because, until recently, almost all our baptismal hymns presupposed infant candidates exclusively. A good case can be made for avoiding such texts, even when some or all of the candidates *are* children: we need to counteract the prevailing assumption that baptism is an infantile rite. Further, most of the singers will be adults who need to develop an adult baptismal spirituality for themselves.

Chants of the Baptismal Rite

The Prayers for the Candidates may be sung to tone 4, BAS page 916. The tones for the Thanksgiving over the Water are found in the Presider's Edition of the BAS pages 29-35.

Chants Within the Rite

It is appropriate for the people to acclaim each new Christian with alleluias, or with some brief anthem as s/he rises from the water; for example:
Songs for a Gospel People (Wood Lake Books, 1987):
    122 — You have put on Christ

ICEL Resource Collection (GIA 1981):
    261 — You are God's work of art
    265 — You have put on Christ

Who Calls You by Name — Music for Christian Initiation: David Haas (GIA 1987):
    p 73 — I am the resurrection
    p 102 — Springs of water, bless the Lord
    p 99 — There is one Lord

Catholic Book of Worship II (CCCB & Gordon V Thompson 1980):
  12 — You are God's work of art
  15 — You have put on Christ

Psalms Within the Rite

Psalm 42
(during the procession to the font):

Songs for a Gospel People (Wood Lake Books, 1987):
  37 — As longs the deer
  89 — As longs the hart

The Hymnal 1982 (Church Hymnal Corporation 1985):
  658 — As longs the deer

Gather (GIA 1988):
  28 — Song of the exile (responsorial)

Psalm 23
(during the vesting of new Christians):

The Hymn Book (ACC & UCC 1971):
  132 — The king of love my shepherd is
  131 — The Lord's my shepherd

Songs for a Gospel People (Wood Lake Books, 1987):
  75 — My shepherd is the living Lord

The Hymnal 1982 (Church Hymnal Corporation 1985):
  664 — My shepherd will supply my need
  645,646 — The king of love my shepherd is
  663 — The Lord my God my shepherd is

ICEL Resource Collection (GIA 1981):
  163 — My shepherd will supply my need

Gather (GIA 1988):
  279 — Because the Lord is my shepherd
  20 — Shepherd me, O God (responsorial)
  274 — The Lord is my shepherd

Catholic Book of Worship II (CCCB & Gordon V Thompson 1980):
   691 — And I will follow
   408 — My shepherd is the Lord (responsorial)
   410 — The Lord is my shepherd (responsorial)
   690 — The living God my shepherd is

Vesting Hymns

The Hymn Book (ACC & UCC 1971):
   313 — Now in the name of him

Songs for a Gospel People (Wood Lake Books, 1987):
   62 — Now there is no male or female

The Hymnal 1982 (Church Hymnal Corporation 1985):
   296 — We know that Christ is raised

ICEL Resource Collection (GIA 1981):
   263 — Rejoice you newly baptized

Glory and Praise (NALR 1984)
   202 — We praise you the Father
   60 — You have been baptized in Christ

Who Calls You by Name — Music for Christian Initiation: David Haas (GIA 1987):
   p 97 — You are God's work of art

In Search of Hope and Grace (GIA 1991):
   p 77 – Servants of the Saviour

New Beginnings (Hope, 1992)
   23 – In Water We Grow

Some of the Taizé chants may be used as well, repeated for as long as appropriate (see Music from Taizé, volumes I & II (GIA 1981 & 1984):
   Bless the Lord (Vol II)
   Confitemini Domino (Vol II, Gather) *
   Jubilate, servite (Vol I, Gather) *
   Laudate Dominum (Vol I, Gather) *
   Laudate omnes gentes (Vol I) *

Laus tibi Christe (Vol II) *
Psallite Deo (Vol II, Gather)
Psallite Domino (Vol II) *
Surrexit Christus (Vol II, Gather) *
Surrexit Dominus Vere II (Vol I, Gather) *
There is one Lord (Vol II)
Tibi Deo (Vol I) *
Ubi Caritas (Vol I, Gather) *

Latin text only

Baptismal Hymns

(in addition to those listed above)

None of the following presupposes infant candidates:

The Hymn Book (ACC & UCC 1971):
    321 — Lift high the cross
    318 — Praise and thanksgiving be to our Creator

Songs for a Gospel People (Wood Lake Books, 1987):
    47 — Rise up O saints of God

The Hymnal 1982 (Church Hymnal Corporation 1985):
    298 — All who believe and are baptized
    294 — Baptized in water
    297 — Descend O Spirit, purging flame
    295 — Sing praise to our Creator
    299 — Spirit of God unleashed on earth

ICEL Resource Collection (GIA 1981):
    263 — Rejoice you newly baptized
    269 — Receive the light of Christ

Gather (GIA 1988):
    298 — Anthem
    332 — Baptized in water
    280 — Bring forth the kingdom
    299 — Now we remain
    242 — O healing river
    309 — Song of the gathering

Catholic Book of Worship II (CCCB & Gordon V Thompson 1980):
　505 — The light of Christ

In Search of Hope and Grace (GIA 1991):
　p 67 — Crashing Waters at Creation
　p 13 — Down Galilee's Slow Roadways

Appendix 3: INTERCESSIONS

Intercessions in the Great Thanksgiving
At a celebration of Baptism, the presider may include intercessions in the Eucharistic Prayer, in the manner of prayer 6 in the BAS. (This is also appropriate in prayers 1 and 2, immediately preceding the final paragraph.)
The following may be used:

Remember, gracious God,
your one holy catholic and apostolic Church,
redeemed by the blood of your Christ.
Reveal its unity, guard its faith,
and preserve it in peace.

Remember N and N who have shared through baptism
the death of your Son.
Reveal in them the glorious resurrection
of Christ our Lord.
[Remember . . .]
[Remember all who have died in the peace of Christ,
and those whose faith is known to you alone;
bring them into the place of eternal joy and light.]

And grant that we may find our inheritance
with [the blessed Virgin Mary,
with patriarchs, prophets, apostles, and martyrs,
(with . . .) and] all the saints
who have found favour with you in ages past.
We praise you in union with them
and give you glory
through your Son Jesus Christ our Lord.

Intercessions after the Peace
As an alternative to intercessions in the Eucharistic Prayer a form of Prayers of the People may follow the exchange of the Peace. In this way, the Peace

remains intimately associated with the baptism as a celebration of the reconciliation accomplished in baptism. A deacon or any baptized person leads the prayers.

Some or all of the following litany may be used or adapted as appropriate. A musical setting may be found in the BAS, page 915, no. 1.

(In peace let us pray to the Lord, saying, "Lord, have mercy.")
For the holy Church of God in every place,
for this parish community, this diocese, and N our bishop,
let us pray to the Lord.
Lord, have mercy.

For all the baptized in their vocation and ministry,
let us pray to the Lord.
Lord, have mercy.

For the welfare of all people, for this nation and its leaders,
for _____,
for this city, and for every city and community,
let us pray to the Lord.
Lord, have mercy.

For the sick and the suffering, the hungry, and the lonely,
for _____, and for those in any need or trouble,
let us pray to the Lord.
Lord, have mercy.

For all who have died in the hope of the resurrection,
especially _____, and for all the departed,
let us pray to the Lord.
Lord, have mercy.

Remembering (...and) all the saints,
we commit ourselves, one another, and our whole life
to Christ our God.
To you, O Lord.

For you anoint our head with oil and spread a table before us,
and to you we give glory, O God, Source of all being, Eternal Word, and Holy Spirit, now and forever. **Amen.**

Appendix 4: THE GIVING OF THE NEW CLOTHES

If a form of words is desired to accompany the giving of the white clothes (similar to the words at the giving of the light), the following may be used.

One of the ministers may give to each of the newly baptized white clothing, saying,
Receive the robe of righteousness
to show that you have put on Christ.

When all of the newly baptized have received new clothing, the people say,
Be clothed in his love
that you may stand without shame or fear
on the day of his appearing.

If these words are to be used, they will need to be printed in a service leaflet; and it may be desirable to print also the words used at the Giving of the Light, and to direct people's attention there when the gifts of light and clothing are to be presented.

Appendix 5:
REFLECTION ON THE EXPERIENCE OF IMMERSION

"I began a personal relationship with God as an adult; reading the Gospel and talking with others about the life of Christ became very exciting to me. In time, I developed a great desire to be baptized and to make the gospel a part of my own daily life.

"Together with my sponsors, during the period of preparation for my baptism, I grew in understanding and confidence within my own Christian life; I also experienced an integration into the church community. I was able to reflect on the baptismal covenant, making it part of my own life, a life that I was now able to share within a welcoming congregation. It was during this time that I realized that at my baptism I wanted plenty of water; I wanted to be fully immersed in the love of Christ.

"My sponsors led me through the actual baptism. When the question was asked, `Do you turn to Christ?' feelings of great joy and peace overwhelmed me. I knew that he was with me as we walked toward the water. I remember, as I stepped into the water, the many people gathered close by to witness what was happening. During the actual immersion, I felt that part of my life was ending and that I could now move into a closer relationship with Christ.

"At the sharing of the Peace, I knew I had become a part of a supportive and loving family within the church. This was further strengthened when I was able to present the gifts for the eucharist; it felt as though I was presenting myself to the congregation and to the life of the church.

"I feel very privileged to have been an adult when reaching the decision to be baptized, and to be fully immersed in the water of baptism. Having an understanding of the Gospel, and feeling a great love for Christ has made my baptism the most awesome experience of my life."

Shirley Griffin, baptized at Pentecost, 1989

Appendix 6: BAPTISMAL POOLS

Sixth century mosaic font in Kelibia, Tunisia.

Fourth century hexagonal font in the baptistry at Poitiers, France.

INTO THE HOUSEHOLD OF GOD

(Top, left) Fifth century octagonal font at Timgad in Numidia, North Africa. Note the three steps.

(Top, right) Early cruciform font in the baptistry of the northern Basilica of Sbaita, south of Beersheba.

(Above) Square font with ceremonial canopy, at Djemila in Numidia, North Africa.

(Left) Sixth century round font in the baptistry at Nocera Superiore, near Capua, Italy.

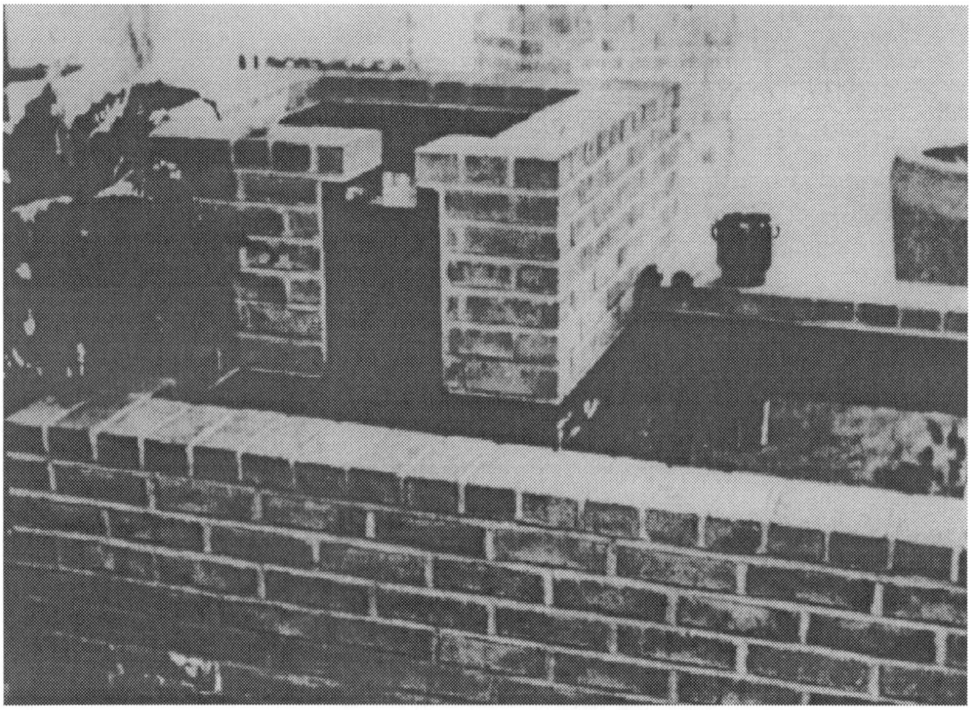

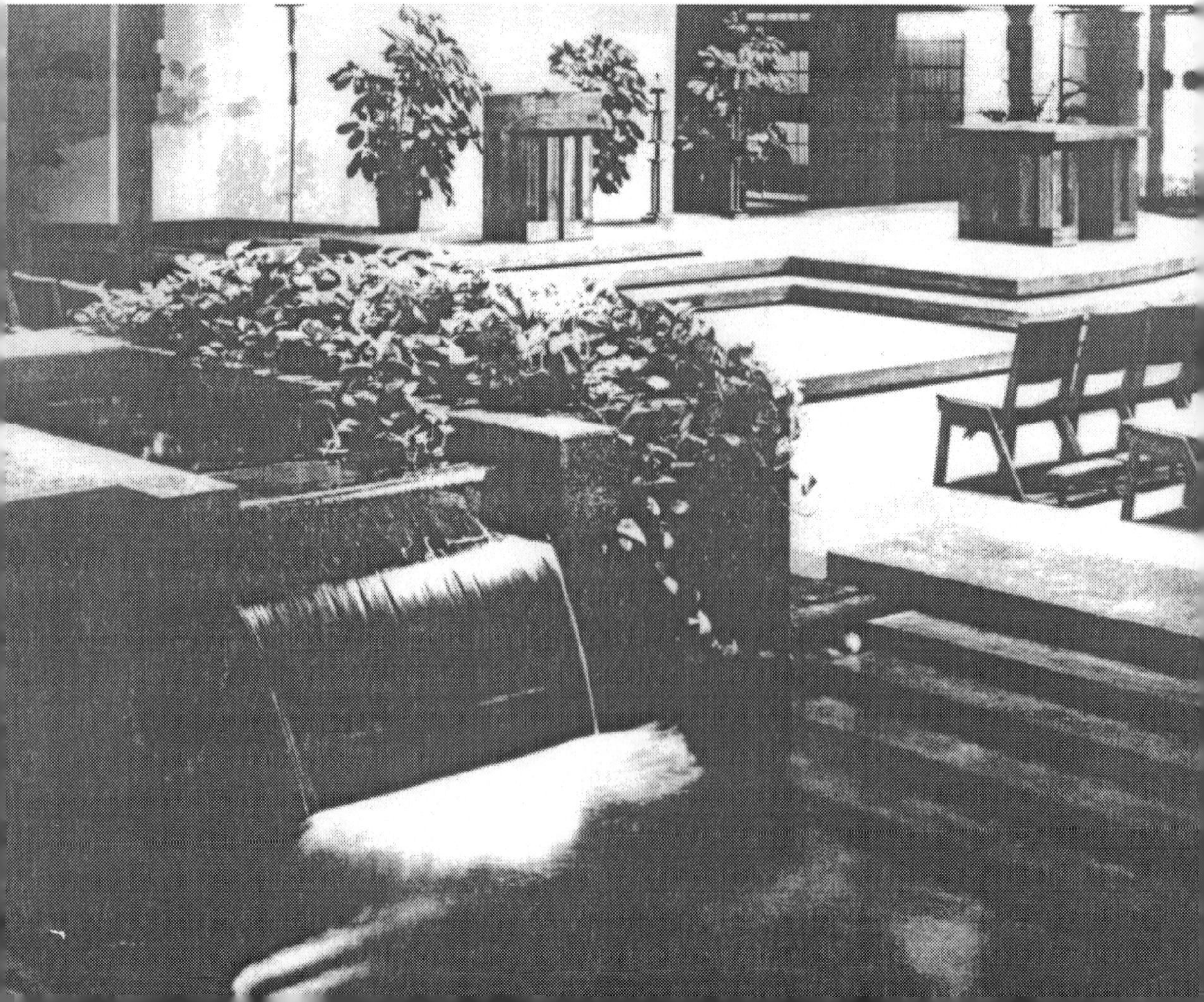

(Opposite page, top) Two-level font at St Margaret's Church in Naperville, Illinois.

(Opposite page, bottom) Font with running water at St Anthony's Church, Kailua, Hawaii.

(Above) Octagonal font at the Church of St. John the Evangelist in Hopkins, Minnesota.

Baptismal pool at the Church of St Benedict the African in Chicago; architect: James Belli.

Appendix 7: PREACHING AT BAPTISM

The context of preaching at baptism makes it a special challenge. There is a wonderful convergence of festival and initiation. There is the temptation on the part of some of us to think of the baptism as "their" intrusion into "our" liturgy. And there are probably many visitors. What follows are merely suggestions about appropriate starting points for preaching on this occasion.

1. Preach on the lectionary. Baptism is a celebration by the baptizing community, not by certain individuals or families; and the liturgical life of the community must be honoured.
2. Preach on the festival as a way of making clear who and what the baptizing community is: we are an Easter people, a Pentecost people, a communion of saints, sharers in the baptism of Jesus, etc. This is the community which incorporates new members into itself.
3. Speak on behalf of the candidates, insofar as you have permission to do so; proclaim the gospel to which they are responding in baptism, giving visitors the opportunity to be clear about the nature of the step these new Christians are taking.
4. Preach about the ways in which baptism illumines the festival and the festival illumines baptism.
5. The sermon at baptism falls at the end of a period of catechetical formation, and launches a new period of mystagogical formation. It can reflect on the candidates' experiences of the journey thus far, and open the door to the exploration of that mystery which now surrounds us in the sacramental life.
6. Coach the community in participating in the great liturgical drama that is about to unfold.
7. Preach the lectionary; it was designed to support and shape this celebration.

Other Hoskin Group Books *in this series*

THINKING ABOUT BAPTISM
John W.B. Hill

ISBN 1-895457-01-7

This widely used booklet is an ideal handout for those who inquire about baptism.

MAKING DISCIPLES
Serving Those Who Are Entering the Christian Life
John W.B. Hill

ISBN 1-895457-02-5

This is a proposal for a restored catechumenate built around the rites and order of the *Book of Alternative Services*. It invites us to rethink the way we prepare people for baptism, and offers substantial resources.

LET US GIVE THANKS
A Presider's Manual for the BAS Eucharist
David Holeton, with Catherine Hall and Gregory Kerr-Wilson
illustrations by Willem Hart

ISBN 1-895457-00-9

A basic 'how-to' book, primarily for presiders, but also helpful for lay readers in the parish. The book 'walks through' the BAS Eucharist, discussing the various activities and how they might be most effectively accomplished. Helpful information on history, shape, and structure, as well as practical details.